imagine

having epilepsy

Linda O'Neill

The Rourke Press, Inc.
Vero Beach, Florida 32964

NOTE: Not all of the children photographed in this book have epilepsy, but volunteered to be
photographed to help raise public awareness.

PHOTO CREDITS
© Eyewire: cover, pages 16, 20, 22; © East Coast Studios: pages 6, 24;
© PhotoDisc: pages 11, 12, 14; © Corel: pages 18, 29

PRODUCED & DESIGNED by East Coast Studios
eastcoaststudios.com

EDITORIAL SERVICES
Pamela Schroeder

Library of Congress Cataloging-in-Publication Data

O'Neill, Linda
    Having epilepsy / Linda O'Neill.
        p. cm — (Imagine...)
    Includes index.
    ISBN 1-57103-381-5
    1. Epilepsy--Juvenile literature. [1. Epilepsy. 2. Diseases.] I. Title. II. Imagine (VeroBeach, Fla.)

RC372.2 .054 2000
616.8'53--dcl

00-029079

Printed in the USA

Author's Note

This series of books is meant to enlighten and give children an awareness and sensitivity to those people who might not be just like them. We all have obstacles to overcome and challenges to meet. We need to think of the person first, not the disability. The children I interviewed for this series showed not one bit of self-pity. Their spirit and courage is admirable and inspirational.

Linda O'Neill

Table of Contents

Imagine This

You open your eyes and you are lying on the floor. You have a bad headache. You feel confused and very tired. Your mom tells you that you had a **seizure** (SEE zhur). You don't remember falling or your body jerking. You know this is what happened because your family has told you. Seizures are a **symptom** (SIMP tom) of **epilepsy** (EP ah LEHP see).

Some seizures make you fall down.

What Is Epilepsy?

Epilepsy means some cells in your brain don't work just right. Your brain tells your body what to do using electrical signals. Your brain has billions of special cells called **neurons** (NEW ronz). Neurons store energy. To send a signal, they "fire" or give off energy. When they give off too much energy or go too fast, the signals get mixed up. You have a seizure.

Your brain has billions of cells called neurons.

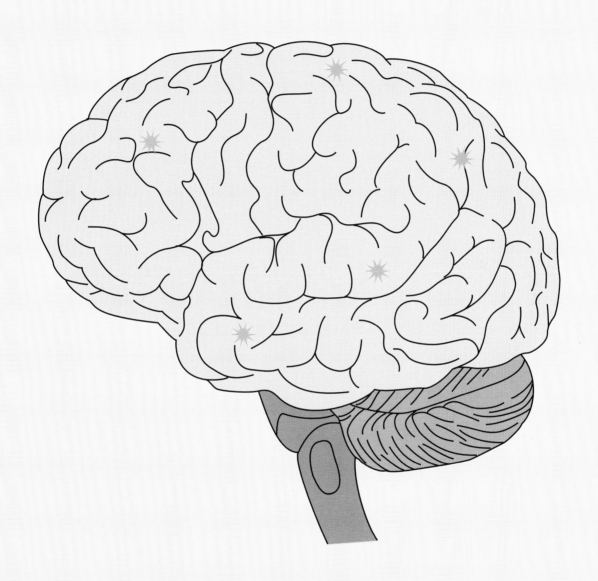

Sometimes your body will warn you. You will get a funny feeling in your head or stomach. You might smell something. This is called an **aura** (AW rah). Having an aura might give you some time to tell your parents or teacher.

Doctors don't know why you might have epilepsy. It might be from a sickness when you were a baby. It might be from an **injury** (IN jer ee) to your head.

Some kids have epilepsy when they are young but don't have it when they get older.

One type of seizure looks like you are daydreaming.

Seizures

There are many types of seizures. One type of seizure may look like you're daydreaming. It only lasts a little while, but you might have it many times a day. You might not even know this is happening. Other seizures can make your arms or legs shake or jerk. Some seizures make you fall. Others do not. You might do silly things or you might look scary during a seizure. You can't help what you do during a seizure.

After a seizure, you may feel confused. You may be very sleepy and have a headache. You may want to sleep for a long time.

After a seizure, you may be tired and confused.

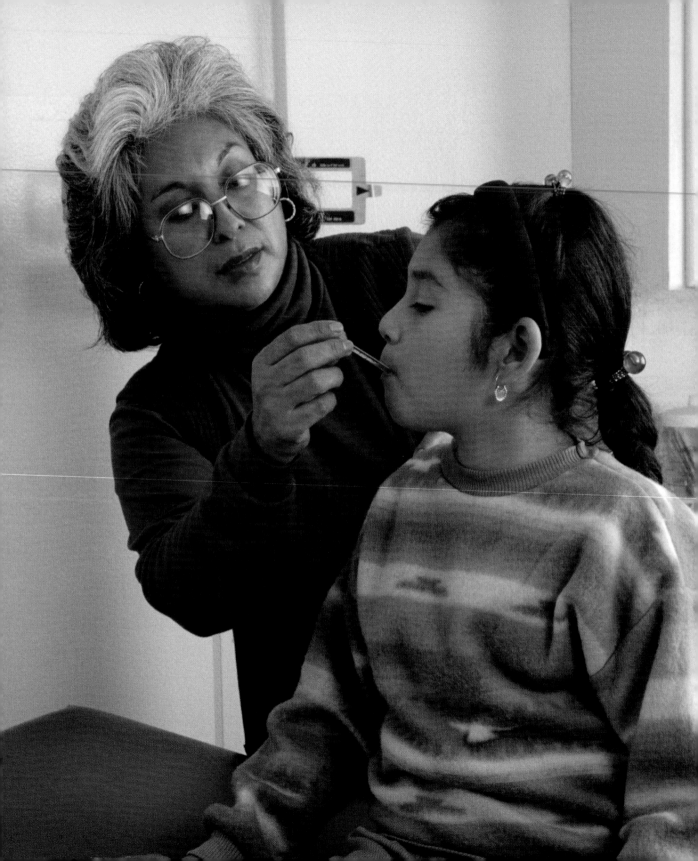

Tests for Epilepsy

Sometimes people who don't have epilepsy have seizures, too. You might have a seizure from a high fever. A fever is when your body temperature is higher than normal. A normal temperature is around 98.6 degrees Fahrenheit (37 degrees celsius).

When children run a very high fever while sick, they may have a seizure. This may be scary for the parents to see, but it does no harm to the child. It is caused by the fever. Once the fever is gone, there are no more seizures.

A normal temperature is 98.6 degrees.

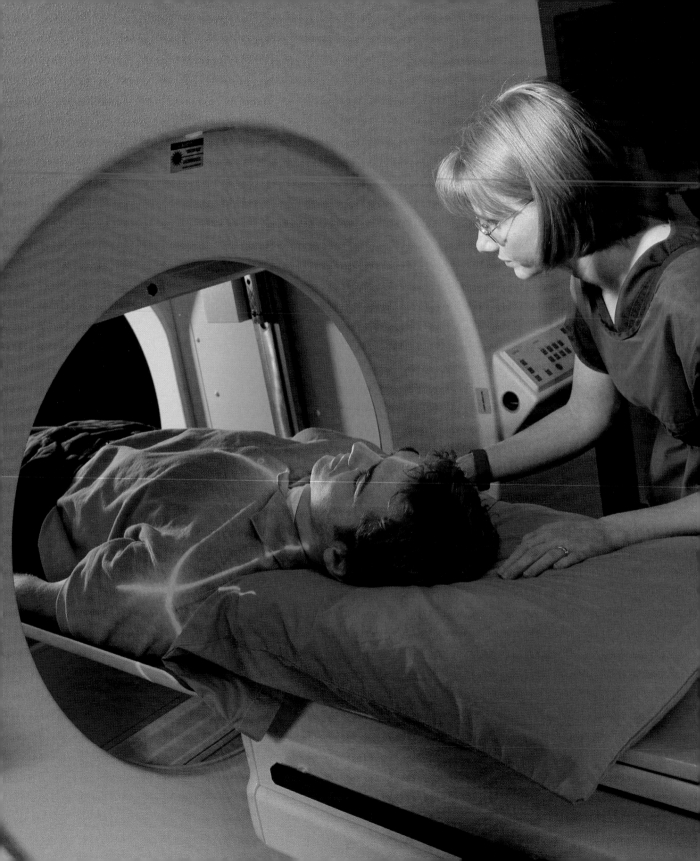

Epilepsy means having more than one seizure. Your doctor can take pictures of your brain with an MRI or a CAT scan. These will show the doctor if you have an injury to your brain. Your doctor also can put wires with sticky pads on your head. Then he or she hooks the wires up to a machine called an EEG. This machine uses special pens and paper to draw a picture of your brain waves. With this picture, your doctor can tell what kind of seizure you are having.

Doctors can take pictures of all parts of your body—even your brain.

Medicine and Diet

There are lots of medicines to help with epilepsy. Your doctor decides what is best. You may have to try different medicines to see which works best for you. The goal is to stop you from having seizures.

Taking the right medicine can help stop seizures.

For some children, a **ketogenic** (KEH toh jen ik) **diet** (DIE et) works best. Doctors are not sure why this diet works, but it stops some children from having seizures. The diet is hard to stay on. You can eat lots of fats but no cookies or cakes! You stay on this diet for two years and then add other foods. Kids who use this diet are called "keto kids."

Getting plenty of sleep is also very important. You are more likely to have a seizure when you are very tired.

A ketogenic diet means no sweets.

Practice Safety

If you know you have epilepsy, you should practice safety at all times. Besides taking your medicine, you should wear a helmet when biking, skating, or climbing. Wear a seat belt in the car. You should always take someone with you when you swim. These safety rules are good things for your friends to do, too!

A Medic Alert bracelet or necklace will tell people you have epilepsy in case you have a seizure.

Wearing a helmet when bike riding is a good safety habit.

Teach Your Friends

Tell your friends about epilepsy:

- You don't catch epilepsy from anyone.
- Epilepsy is not a mental problem.
- You can't swallow your tongue when you are having a seizure.
- You can't help what you do during a seizure.
- Even though it looks scary, you are not in pain.
- You might be a little embarrassed when you come out of the seizure.

A medic alert necklace can tell doctors and nurses you have epilepsy.

Tell your friends what they can do if they see you having a seizure:

- Don't try to stop the seizure.
- Take away things that could hurt you.
- Protect your head with a pillow or something soft.
- Roll you onto your side after the seizure is done.
- Don't offer you anything to eat or drink until you are fully awake.

Meet Someone Special!

Meet Steve

How old were you when you had your first seizure?

"I don't know."

What kind of seizures did you have?

"My teachers thought I wasn't paying attention in class. My mom thought I was tuning her out. That kind of seizure is called an absence seizure."

Do you take medicine for epilepsy?

"I do now. Once I started having seizures that people knew were seizures."

Do you still have seizures?

"No, the medicine I take has stopped the seizures. I haven't had a seizure in 8 months."

What kind of tests did you have?

"I had an MRI and a CAT scan."

27

Did the tests show anything?

"I don't know."

Does having epilepsy make you feel different from other kids?

"Sometimes. It's embarrassing to know you've had a seizure and don't know what you did. It still makes me nervous to not know if it will happen again."

What would you like other kids to know about epilepsy?

"That they shouldn't be scared if I have a seizure."

What do you want to do when you get older?

"I want to be a coach for basketball. I hope I can drive a car."

Staying safe means never swimming alone.

Glossary

aura (AW rah) — a certain feeling all around you

diet (DIE et) — eating special foods

epilepsy (EP ah LEHP see) — a disorder of brain cells

injury (IN jer ee) — damage to the body, a hurt

ketogenic diet (KEH toh jen ik DIE et) — a diet having more fat than protein or carbohydrates

neurons (NEW ronz) — brain cells that receive and send messages to your body

seizure (SEE zhur) — a sudden attack

symptom (SIMP tom) — a sign

Further reading

Gosselin, Kim. *Taking Seizure Disorders to School: A Story About Epilepsy,* Jay Jo Books, 1998

Landau, Elaine. *Epilepsy (Understanding Illness),* Twenty First Century Books, 1995

Visit these Websites
www.efa.org

Index